The
DINKUM AUSSIE DICTIONARY

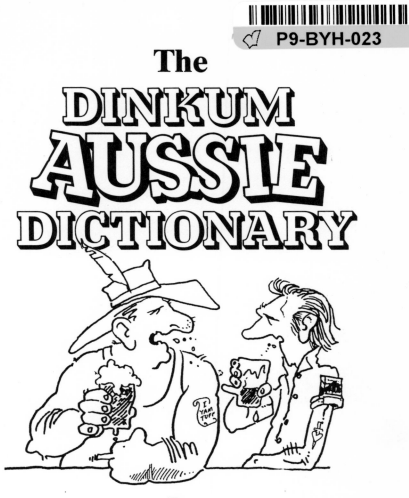

By
Crooked Mick of the Speewa

Illustrated by Brendan Akhurst

A Dinkum Aussie Publication

C&H CHILD & HENRY AUSTRALIA

A Bex, a nice cup of tea, a cry and a good lie down: A somewhat archaic phrase, usually directed by a woman friend to a woman sufferer. In the past the victim's husband would have usually just beaten her up and stolen her housekeeping money to get on the grog and go to the races. In these trying times the victim will have usually innocently discovered that her husband has turned gay. The amazing Bex headache powder, not being what it once was, due to changes in the pharmaceutical laws of the land, is no longer of much use. The victim is normally advised to skip the cry and lie down as well, and flee simultaneously to her lawyer and the nearest women's refuge.

A bit strong: A hurtful remark or action, viz., 'Well, I can understand him pissing off with your missus, but taking the dog as well, now that was *a bit strong.*'

Abo: Short for Aborigine; a derisory and insulting term.

About right: Means that the statement/fact is absolutely correct. The phrase is an excellent example of the average Australian's refusal or inability to admit anything being true except in an indirect manner. Thus the reply to the classic phrase, 'I think therefore I am,' is: 'That'd be *about right*, mate.'

Aerial pingpong: Australia's home-devised football code, Australian

3

All dressed up and nowhere to go:

Rules. Incomprehensible to civilised races, it makes about as much sense as the equally dubious sport of water polo.

Alf: A fool.

All dressed up and nowhere to go: The person referred to as being in this state has made a mistake about the time of a plane departure, the day of the party, a sure thing for the races or even the fact that the world cared about him or her. In male parlance it means that one has been 'stood up' by one's *sheila*. A failure.

Ankle biter: A form of *rug rat*. A member of the human race, of indeterminate sex and of any colour, under two years old.

Apeshit: Stark raving mad, usually in the noun form, viz., 'He's *apeshit* today.'

Arse about with care: Means that things have gone wrong because some fool has tried to help. In other words the building is not only a gutted ruin but the members of the local fire brigade have destroyed the remnants with their hoses.

Arse into gear: One had better do this if one is not about to get *arseholed*. The necessity of at least appearing to do some work while the boss is around.

Arseholed: Has nothing to do with the Americanism 'arsehole' which means a fool or a curmudgeon and everything to do with losing one's job (if a bricklayer) or being thrown out of a pub (if one is a lower-order drunk who is *arseholed*). Chairmen of Directors do not get *arseholed* from their jobs; they are sacked. Likewise, they are thrown out of public houses. There are certain fine points of language in this egalitarian society.

As useful as...: A starting phrase that can precede almost any collection of words meaning that the person concerned is not pulling his or her weight and is making no useful contribution to the philosophical discussion at hand. Thus, '*as useful as* a wether at a ram sale', '*as useful as* tits on a bull', '*as useful as* an ashtray on a motor bike' and '*as useful as* a dead dingo's donger'.

Back of Beyond: The interior of Australia, but used in a rather wistful sense as in, '*Back of Beyond* where a man can feel free', or some such rubbish. Invariably uttered by a city dweller who would die of thirst and heatstroke if he attempted to leave the inner suburbs.

Baked Dinner:

Bad way: One is in a *bad way* if one is suffering from a hangover or has been recently run over by a double-decker bus.

Baked dinner: Once the traditional Sunday midday meal, consisting of a roast leg of lamb, roast and mashed spuds, roast pumpkin, carrot and parsnip, peas, brown gravy and mint sauce. Prepared by the expert hands of the average Australian housewife it was once guaranteed to *choke a brown dog.*

Balmain bug: A tasty and good-looking crustacean related to the lobster and the true crayfish. A shining example of the Australian inability to give good food a pleasant name. In a displaced burst of northern nationalism, Queenslanders insist on calling the wretched animal the Moreton Bay bug.

Bangs like a dunny door: Used by males in reference to any female of the species who is said to be free with her sexual favours. It invariably turns out to be a lie.

Barbie: A barbecue meal, cooked on a hotplate or over hot coals. Regarded with universal scorn by those who slaver over *bistecca alla Fiorentina*, which is exactly the same thing apart from the fact that it is done indoors and served by some whacker wearing a dinner jacket.

Barcoo rot: A form of scurvy caused by the bushworker's diet of corned beef and damper.

Barrack: To encourage one's team from the sidelines, not always in complimentary terms, e.g., 'Get in there and fight, you bunch of bloody pansies.'

Basketweaver from Balmain: A trendy, basically middle class, upwardly mobile, socially conscious, left-wing member of the Australian Labor Party and one who has no intention of manning the barricades for any cause whatsoever. Derisory.

Bastard: Either a term of affection as in, 'good old *bastard*', a term of abuse as in, '*bloody bastard*', or a comment on the weather as in, '*bastard* of a day', meaning that it is either hot or cold. The Australian male uses the word indiscriminately in place of almost any other in the English language, thus:
> So I told the flash *bastard* I wasn't going to do his *bastard* of a job on a *bastard* of a day like this. But the *bastard* told me I had no *bloody* choice. I did it and he turned out not to be a bad old *bastard* in the end. But it was still a *bastard* of a job.

The one meaning that the word does not carry in Australian usage is its officially defined one concerning the legitimacy of one's birth. In general 'flash *bastard*' means a smartarse, 'good old *bastard*' is a close friend and 'poor old *bastard*' applies to a person of the grandfather class who is down on his luck.

Bastard from the bush: Mythical folk hero celebrated in (mainly) smutty jingles and at least one long, sub-literate poem. The *bastard from the bush* is one of life's great swine and, because of this, tolerated with great affection by Australian males.

Battler: A male who has had a hard life and will continue to have one due to unforeseen circumstances, his own stupidity or both. *Battlers* are generally hard workers of abstemious habits but these twin decencies never get them anywhere.

Bazz/Bazza: Originally a cartoon character but now taken to mean your average, knockabout, sub-literate Australian bloke. More or less a fool.

Beak: A judge.

Beats watering the garden: A pleasantry uttered by one who has been engulfed by a flood.

Beaut: Very good or excellent. Normally used in the phrases, 'you *beaut*', 'you bloody *beaut*', or the television corruption, 'bewdie'.

Better than a poke in the eye with a burnt stick: Things have turned out better than expected but in a backhanded sort of way, i.e., the car, by some miracle, has not been repossessed and one's house has not burnt down.

Big smoke: A country expression for any large city.

Billabong: A waterhole formed by a broken meander of a river.

Billy: The name of a friend or a pot for boiling water for tea over an open fire. In the case of the former it must not be black. In the case of the latter it has to be. A shiny billy makes awful tea.

Billy-oh: A somewhat archaic word that can either mean that one has had a wonderful time at a party or that one is feeling more than slightly off-colour or sick; thus, 'I played up like *billy-oh*', last night or, 'my rheumatism is playing up like *billy-oh*.' One's rheumatism, sciatica or mild case of clap can also be, 'giving one *billy-oh*'. One can also give the neighbour's unpleasant dog *billy-oh* which translates into the fact that one has beaten the wretched animal half to death with a pick handle.

Bitzer: A dog consisting of many breeds, a mongrel. A bit of this and a bit of that.

Black bastard: A term of endearment used to describe Australia's only home-bred dog strain, other than the disputed kelpie, officially known as the blue heeler, Queensland blue or Queensland cattle dog. All blues are regarded by their owners as being 'as thick as two bricks' but 'as game as Ned Kelly'. They are also renowned for their biting ability.

Black Maria: A prison cell on four wheels that, if necessary, can travel at high speeds. In the past most of its business was done outside pubs on Saturday nights. These days its customers in the main come from the street demonstration set.

Black Stump: The official signpost at the beginning of nowhere. A solid version of the Styx which lacks Charon as a ticket collector. Anyone who lives 'beyond the *Black Stump*' is regarded as being stark, raving mad.

Blind Freddy: A mythical and dull person who can understand matters intellectual only if they are hammered into his skull by a railway fettler using an old-fashioned 10-inch spike. Thus, 'Even *Blind Freddy* could tell you', that the government would fall, that the river was about to flood, etc.

Bloke: A male Australian, a 'cove'. Some *blokes* are 'good coves', others are 'right *bastards*'.

Bloodhouse: An unsavoury hotel.

Bloody: Once the great Australian adjective, in these intellectual times it has been supplanted by a four letter word with '-ing' attached which describes the act of fornication. Frequently used in conjunction with *bastard*, it is also inserted in sentences where that word makes even less sense than it normally does. Often used to emphasise that something is particularly good thus, '*bloody* good feed/fight/day/night/party/dog/horse/wife/child/lounge suite/budgie.'

Blotto: Dead drunk; intoxicated to the extreme.

Blowie: A blowfly.

Blow-in: An unexpected and not particularly welcome guest: 'He's just a bloody *blow-in*; tell him to go to buggery.'

Bludge: To loaf. 'Having a *bludge*' is an integral part of the Australian workingman's life.

Bludger: In theory one who lives on the earnings of a prostitute. In actual fact still the worst insult that can be offered a man in Australia, hence, dole *bludger*. This expression is usually mouthed by members of the violent right in this country against anyone not of their political opinion.

Blue heeler: See *Black bastard*.

Bluey: A bedroll containing clothing and other odds and ends carried by a swagman, also known as a *swag* or *Matilda*. It, because of the colour, is also a parking ticket issued by a traffic policeman.

Bob's yer uncle: Everything is 'Jake' or OK. Thus the Australian reply to a NASA official's query as to the possibility of a space-shuttle lift-off would be: '*Bob's yer uncle*, mate.' As this would cause some confusion, Australians by and large are banned from verbal roles in free world space scenarios.

Bodgie: Once an unwholesome species of lower-order male street life in the 1950s (the female version being a 'Widgie'). Now used only as part of the phrase 'a *bodgie* job' or 'to *bodgie* up', meaning that a highly specialised piece of electronic equipment has been lashed together with fencing wire or anything else that happened to be lying around the toolshed at the time.

Bog in: An invitation to sit down at the dinner table and delicately partake of the excellent comestibles prepared by one's hostess.

Bomb out: To fail…'I had a go at the job but I *bombed out*.'

Bonzer: *Grouse* or good. After *bogging in* one can thank one's hostess by declaring, 'That was a *bonzer* feed, that was.'

Boofhead: A former cartoon character noted for his thickness. In general terms, a dullard.

Boomer: A large male kangaroo; otherwise something good, i.e., 'That was a real *boomer*.'

Boong: Derogatory term for an Aborigine.

Bottom of the harbour: A scheme by which companies were manipulated to thwart the Deputy Commissioner of Taxation of money that was rightfully the property of the Australian federal government. In the 1970s people who ran *bottom of the harbour* schemes were regarded by certain sections of the business community as national heroes. They still are.

Bower bird: An Australian native bird that decorates its home with useless glittering items in an effort to entice a female bower bird to share his life. In human terms the description retains its essential accuracy.

Brass razoo: Worthless item. An object is said to be, 'not worth a *brass razoo*'. *Brass razoos* are enthusiastically collected by *bower birds*.

Brumby: A wild horse, which is an integral component of Australia's canned dogfood industry and the advertising business, which, for some peculiar reason, uses herds of brumbies to advertise soap powder and cigarettes.

Bucket: To criticise or in turn be criticised. One can *bucket* an adversary or, in one's turn, 'be *bucketed*' by the self same person.

Buckjumper: A rodeo horse that jumps up and down to earn its daily hay ration for reasons which it itself cannot understand.

Buckley's: In unpleasant situations one always has two chances, one's own and Buckley's which means that one has no chance whatsoever. No one knows for sure who the mythical Buckley was but he definitely was *dead-set* unlucky. The name of the Melbourne firm, Buckley and Nunn, is another suggested derivation. Always used in the phrase, 'You've got two chances, mate, yours and *Buckley's*.'

Budgie: An idiotic and small member of the parrot family native to Australia's arid regions much loved as pets by elderly women. With patience *budgies* can be taught almost as many tricks as company directors, doctors and lawyers.

Bugger: Sometimes a substitute for bastard inasmuch as one can be a mean old *bugger* or a good old *bugger*. One can also have '*bugger* all' (nothing) or be told to 'go to buggery' (to piss off). As with *bastard* it can also be a *bugger* of a day or a *bugger* of a job. Unlike *bastard*, however, one can be '*buggered*' (exhausted) or '*buggered* about' (given a hard time by one's mates or employer). The word has absolutely nothing to do with its (Oxford) derivation of a heretic from Bulgaria or a sodomite.

Bull artist: Short for bullshit artist. An unpleasant liar who is much given to personal boasting about his cleverness. A member of federal parliament.

Bulldust: Fine dust that covers vehicle tracks and potholes in the interior of the continent. Also something worthless or a lie as in, 'That's a *bloody* load of *bloody bulldust*, mate.'

Bullocky: One in charge of a bullock waggon. Traditionally bullockies were given to hard swearing although why these worthies should be singled out as distinct from the remainder of the male population of the time must forever remain a mystery.

Bull's roar: Insulting expression indicating failure, normally on the sporting field. If something doesn't come within a *bull's roar* of something else, it can be judged to have 'missed by a mile'. Most Australian expressions of this nature have resisted metrication.

Bumper: A cigarette butt. However, a bumper harvest is not one of fag ends.

Bung on a blue: To 'stack on a turn'; with women an attack of hysterics, with men a fist fight. If women *bung on a blue* by throwing plates or knives they invariably 'turn on the waterworks'. Men, on the other hand, are not supposed to cry.

Bunghole: Cheese.

Bunging it on: To 'stack on side'. More or less to act out of one's own class in the upwardly mobile sense. For instance, if one's host, who is normally given to providing his guests with *fourpenny dark* out of Vegemite glasses, suddenly offers a proper champagne out of equally proper glasses he is said to be *bunging it on* or '*bunging on side*'. *Bunging it on* is much frowned upon.

Bunyip: A legendary beast of the bush, well known to the Aborigines and early white explorers. Now largely replaced by the 'Nullarbor Nymph' and panthers of various colours. In the Antipodean sense it falls into the same category as the Loch Ness Monster, the Himalayan Yeti and the North American Wendigo.

Bush: An unkempt area of scraggly ground covered with useless gumtrees. Most Australians have as little as possible to do with the bush although they lyingly claim that this is the area where their hearts belong. However, to 'go *bush*' means that one has fled civilisation because of the pressing demands of one's creditors. In a secondary sense it means to have gone mad.

Bushweek: A situation where everything is a *bloody* mess when it shouldn't be, or where something has gone wrong and the perpetrator of the action is taking advantage of the person making the charge: 'What do you think this is, *bloody bushweek*?' A phrase much used in the country's armed services which normally operate on Murphy's Law (if something is going to go wrong, everything is going to go wrong).

Cadge: To beg, borrow or steal but in a friendly sort of way. Thus a *cadger* is a cut above the universally despised 'bot'. Cadgers normally ask for things that don't really matter, i.e., 'Can I *cadge* a rollie?', which translates as, 'Can I have the necessary ingredients to make myself a roll-your-own-cigarette?'

Camp as a row of tents: A raving queer, poofter or shirt lifter. A homosexual male.

Cheese and Kisses: The missus. One's wife.

Chesty Bond: A former cartoon and advertising character who specialised in sleeveless singlets and male underwear in general. He was good looking, generally decent and kind to women, children and dogs. Universally

◊ **Choke a brown dog:**

despised by the average Australian male who allows his missus to buy his underwear and ties.

Chiack: One is *having a go* at one's mate. To indulge in a mild form of sarcasm. Normally used in the responsive or negative sense thus, 'Stop *chiacking* me, will you, you *bloody bastard.*'

Choke a brown dog: Almost anything nasty will *choke a brown dog.* However, black dogs and black and white dogs seem impervious to various types of culinary poisoning. The phrase normally goes, 'Jeez (a euphemism for Jesus), that pie was as *rough as guts* it would *choke a brown dog*, it would.' Why brown dogs in Australia are more susceptible to ptomaine poisoning than those of a different colour remains a mystery.

Chunder: A *technicolour yawn*. To vomit.

Coathanger: The Sydney Harbour Bridge.

Cobber: One's mate or true friend. The word has not been used in its country of origin for more years than any care to remember. But it is wildly overused by Australians when greeting one another in foreign parts. It takes the form of, 'G'day *cobber*, let's go and have a couple of snorts for old times sake.' Dead drunk, the pair of them go back to the motel to meet the missus who by this stage is climbing up the wall. In other words they are very drunk indeed and she is extremely annoyed. In the past one's *cobber* could be a dead crayfish on a string which one took on a tram and paid its fare. Boiled crayfish, however, were very reluctant *cobbers*.

Cockatoo: A large, white, sulphur-crested parrot, with a raucous voice, native to the country. In popular parlance, a sentinel at an illegal gambling game who keeps an eye open for the *coppers*.

Cocky: In modern useage a farmer of any sort, social standing or wealth. In the nineteenth and early part of this century it was a derisory term for a smallholder (50 hectares or thereabouts), who got everything wrong, was mean, and starved his workmen half to death. These days *cockies* remain at liberty to starve themselves but industrial law prevents them starving the farmhands.

Cocky on the biscuit tin: An extremely complicated expression which, visually, owes its origin to the rosella parrot eating a Sao as shown on large tins of Arnott's biscuits. Arnotts use the rosella as a trademark. The literal translation is rhyming slang for 'on the outside looking in'. Used by members of the rank and file of any union when their elected representatives are engaged in wage discussions with the management and they haven't the slightest idea of what is going on, thus: 'Out here like the *bloody cocky on the bloody biscuit tin.*'

· **Cocky's cage:** One is said to have 'a mouth like the bottom of a *cocky's cage*' when one is suffering from a terminal hangover.

Cocky's Joy: Golden syrup. The only cheap sweetening available to a cocky or farmer in the early days of settlement because jam cost too much (even the wretched melon and lemon). Misery on a selection (land grant) is explained in the following saying: 'The river flooded, me horse dropped dead, the damned wet dog got into me bedding and the ants got into me *Cocky's Joy.*'

Colliwobbles: One can have a 'case of the *colliwobbles*' if one is 'crook in the guts', i.e., sick.

Come up smelling of roses: To extricate one's self from a difficult situation without getting into the shit. A piece of good luck.

Compo: To be 'on *compo*' means to be on workers' compensation, that is receiving a temporary disability pension for injuries received at one's workplace.

Cooee: A supposed call of recognition in the bush invented by early nineteenth century travelling journalists visiting Australia to enliven their otherwise dull copy.

Cop this, young 'Arry: Archaic phrase used by comedian Roy Rene when he was about to punch someone in the ear. A warning that something unpleasant is about to occur.

Copper: A policeman.

Copping it sweet: Taking things easy; having a quiet and pleasant day with a case of beer and a bag of prawns.

Cossie: A swimming costume, as in, 'Hold on a jiff until I get me *cossie* on.'

Couldn't: The start of a number of derogatory phrases, i.e., '*couldn't* catch a cold', '*couldn't* lie straight in bed', '*couldn't* train a choko vine to grow up a dunny wall'... meaning that the person in question is both stupid and untrustworthy.

Cow: The phrase 'a fair *cow*' means that things are crook, thus it can be a 'fair *cow* of a day'. Likewise, 'a *cow* of a job' means that the job is crook. One can also have 'a *cow* of a missus'. The amiable bovine is much maligned in the Australian language.

Crack hardy: To act in a courageous manner or to put up with conditions of extreme hardship when one would much prefer a glass of rum in a quiet, warm place.

Cranky: Bad-tempered, mad or both. Normally used in conjuction with *bloody* and *bastard*, thus, 'He's a *cranky bloody bastard* he is.'

Crawler: Someone who is 'lower than a snake's belly'. A person who fawns upon a superior in the hope of obtaining present or future favours.

Creeping Jesus: A man of the cloth; a clergyman who preaches the teachings of Christ.

Crook as Rookwood: Near to death; Rookwood being a cemetery in the city of Sydney. The word *crook* by itself merely means that one is slightly off colour, usually due to a hangover. On the other hand *'crook* in the guts' is the universal male expression for being genuinely sick due to an abdominal upset.

Crooked as a dog's hind leg: A person who is not to be trusted.

Crooked Mick of the Speewa: A home-grown mythical Australian bush hero who has been replaced, thanks to international television, by various American upstarts. In keeping with Australian male tradition, Crooked Mick, apart from being able to do anything better than anyone else, was also a sometime thief, a drunkard and a liar. The *Speewa* itself was a mythical sheep station generally located on the New South Wales side of the Murray River, although it was sometimes moved to Queensland along with Crooked Mick himself to add to the authenticity of the lie or yarn being told.

Cruel: To *cruel* something is to spoil the chances of another or generally bugger things up by which means one has 'cruelled it'.

Crust: One's manner of making money, hence the query, 'What do you do for a *crust,* mate?'

D: A detective as in, 'The bloody *Ds* are poking round again.'

Dag: Sheep droppings, usually caught in the sheep's wool. 'Cutting out the *dags*' is a term used by shearers when crutching sheep at the beginning of summer to prevent flystrike. The word is also used as a term of insult as in, 'He's a *dag*', meaning that the person (usually male in female terms) is dull, boring and decidedly untrendy. In American slang, a wimp.

Damper: An appalling sort of bread, devised out of sheer necessity by early white settlers and explorers, now sold at wildly inflated prices in equally appalling 'Colonial style' restaurants. It consists of a flour and water dough paste flung into the filthy ashes of an eucalypt fire. The results are indescribable. It was normally eaten with a pannikin of rum and a slice of half-bad corned beef. Nowadays fools are seen dunking it in perfectly edible beef and burgundy to the peril of that dish.

Dead Heart: The centre of Australia which early explorers believed was filled with water. Many of them suffered severely for this misconception.

Dead marine: An empty beer bottle, but definitely not an empty aluminium beer can.

Dead set: A racing term meaning that the horse is an absolute or *dead set* certainty to win the race. The statement is invariably untrue, as is almost all racing advice.

Delicate as a starved dingo: The person referred to has appalling table manners. 'She picked at her food about as *delicately as a starved dingo*.' The Australian native wild dog or dingo is not noted for its good behaviour at mealtimes.

Demon: A police officer. Rarely used in the singular sense mainly because decent gentlemen, quietly minding their own business in a public bar, are usually set upon unfairly and unjustly by a large number of *demons*. Gradually being supplanted by the Americanism, 'pigs'.

Dero: A derelict or down-and-outer who is also probably on the 'turps' or 'meths'. Both terms are used for methylated spirits (taken in refined circles with a dash of fruit cordial to cut the taste). In the good old days if the *demons* caught the *dero* in a public park they would *vag* him (that is arrest and charge him under the Vagrancy Act as having no visible means of support). This method of getting one's arrest tallies up for the month, and thus earning promotion the easy way by persecuting the dispossessed of this earth, is now illegal in most States much to the fury of the 'wallopers'.

Dickhead: A person of no consequence. A fool. One's boss is invariably a *dickhead*.

Didn't come down in the last shower: An Australian version of the expression 'I wasn't born yesterday you know.' Sometimes 'pull the other leg, it rings' is substituted. The remark is made after hearing a barefaced lie by one who hopes to gain financial advantage from telling the untruth.

Digger: Initially one who took part in the gold rushes in New South Wales and Victoria in the nineteenth century. Now the term for an Australian foot soldier under the rank of corporal. This second meaning come into general currency during World War I on the redoubts to Gallipoli. At the time the members of the opposing Turkish army were at a loss to understand why Australians were willing to needlessly sacrifice their lives for perfidious Albion. These days the few remaining survivors are at an equal loss. However, they strongly object to the feminist legions of Women Against Rape marching on Anzac Day (25 April), which commemorates Gallipoli, reasoning, 'They should march on their own *bloody* day.' National Rape Day has yet to be officially gazetted.

Dill: A *bloody* fool.

Ding dong: An imprompu and spontaneous bout of fisticuffs involving a large number of participants of either sex. *Ding dongs* used to be regarded in an affectionate manner but have now been replaced by the deadly serious sporting riot.

Dingbat: Someone with *kangaroos in his or her top paddock*. Crazy but not dangerously so.

Dingo: A native dog of rather clean appearance and habits (apart from at mealtimes). In human parlance, a swine or a *bastard*. In semi-jocular fashion an unexpected dinner guest, in certain stratas of society, can be greeted with the remark, 'Did they forget to feed the bloody *dingoes* then?'

Dingo's breakfast: A piss and a good look round; in other words none at all.

Dinki Di: True blue; on the level. The absolute truth.

Dinkum: Absolutely authentic as in the expression, '*Fair dinkum* mate, I wouldn't lie to you now would I?' The answer to this is, of course, yes.

Dip my lid: To take off one's hat to someone; a salute not necessarily to a woman out of politeness. One can dip one's lid (metaphorically speaking)

Dingo's breakfast:

to a male who has performed some generous or courageous act. The phrase is going out of fashion due to the decline in male headgear.

Dip out: To renege; to refuse to participate. Mainly used in public bars as in, 'I'll *dip out* on this one,' meaning that one does not want a drink.

Dirty: Has two meanings as in, 'I'm *dirty* on him,' meaning annoyed and 'Don't do the dirty on me,' meaning don't let me down or double cross me.

Do your block: Normally preceded by the word, 'don't'. A warning to a friend or enemy not to lose one's temper or start throwing punches. The phrase, 'Don't do your 'nana', can be substituted.

Dob: To incriminate someone as in, 'The bastard *dobbed* me in to the *bloody coppers.*'

Dog: An ugly woman.

Dogger: A professional dingo hunter who makes a living by killing wild dogs for the bounty on their scalps.

Doggo: To 'lie *doggo*' means that one is keeping quiet about matters and attempting to remain inconspicuous.

Dogs are barking: A hot racecourse tip as in, 'Everyone know's he's got a chance, all the *bloody dogs are barking.*'

Dog's dinner: The person or object referred to is unkempt, untidy or a mess.

Dole bludger: Someone who is resting at the expense of the State due to the fact that he or she cannot find employment. Very rich people, who stand to the right of the soup spoon in Australian politics, delude themselves into believing that there is plenty of work for anyone who wants to look for it. Thus anyone who is on the dole is automatically a bludger.

Done like a dinner: To be worsted or badly beaten either in a fist fight or a business deal. A horse that loses a race can also be *done like a dinner*.

Doover: Anything that one cannot get hold of one's self while the tractor is blowing up. Thus, 'For Christ's sake hand me that *doover* will yez?' The recipient of this information will invariably hand the person in question the wrong *doover* and the tractor will explode. International translations are doodad and thingummyjig.

Dose: Short form of 'dose of the shits'. Normally applied to a person that one dislikes, thus, 'He gives me a *dose.*'

Down the drain: Things have turned out for the worse. The horse has lost the race and therefore one's money is *down the drain*. Sometimes expressed as 'down the gurgler' which is a drain by another name.

Down the hatch: An expression uttered before taking a beer with a mate. The expression, *here's looking at you sideways* is equally appropriate and proper on these social occasions because when drinking, one does normally have to observe one's friend in this fashion.

Drack: Dowdy in one's personal attire.

Drag the chain: A person is said to be *dragging the chain* if he is either loafing on the job or not drinking fast enough. To loaf on the job is acceptable but to fall behind in a drinking school is regarded as a crime.

Dreg: An unkempt person of either sex; someone who is both boring and not upwardly mobile. The word is much used by females in reference to a male, who, in international terms, can be described as an arsehole.

Drink with the flies: A person who is an outcast of society, or otherwise disliked by society, is said to *drink with the flies* because they are his only companions.

Drongo: A stupid person; an idiot.

Droob: A fool.

Dropped his bundle: Basically a literary reference to throwing one's swag into the bushes, giving one's dog to the local butcher and then hanging one's self from the handy beam of a nearby shanty (after carefully removing one's boots). In short, to give up and admit failure in this vale of tears which some people call life.

Drover's dog: An inoffensive animal that for many years went about its job quietly which, basically, was ankle-tapping cattle. Then in the early 1980s it learned, to its own intense surprise, that it was capable of winning elections and governing the country. Despite the fact that it lowered its social status the dog *showed willing* and is now governing Australia in a capable fashion.

Drum: The good oil; the truth.

Dry as an old lady's talcum powder: The feminist version of an offensive phrase used by males, i.e., 'dry as a nun's nasty'. The bisexual phrase is 'dry as a dead dingo's donger'. All three expressions mean that the person in question is in desperate need of an alcoholic drink.

Dry blanket: A hot afternoon or day hence, 'It's like a bloody *dry blanket* in here today.'

Duckshove: To avoid responsibility; to push an unpleasant task into the lap of another.

Duds: Male clothing, as in, 'Get your *duds* on and we'll go out and get on the piss and pick up a couple of sheilas.' Females don't wear duds, they are clothed either in frocks or outfits.

Duff: If one *duffs* cattle one steals them. If a woman is 'up the *duff*' she is pregnant. But if one is a *duffer* one is a bloody fool. The word defies further analysis.

Dull as dishwater: The person being spoken of, is.

Dumper: A large wave that picks up a body surfer and slams him into the bottom of the beach, causing joy to the medical profession and terror to his medical insurance company.

Dunderhead: A fool.

Dungaree settler: Archaic. An early member of the now international blue jeans set who settled in the Hawkesbury River area of the infant colony of New South Wales. Most were poor and the survivors quickly became inbred. In short, a term of derision similar to the Americanism 'cracker white'.

Dunny: An outside lavatory or bog whch has given rise to the following famous jingle:
>Don't sit upon
>The dunny seat
>The crabs in here
>Can jump six feet.

This is a non-metricated version of the fact that lavatory seats in public toilets are infested with the whimsical and amusing crab louse. 'Dunnican' was a pan removed once a week by a specially trained 'dunnican man' at the dead of night in non-sewered metropolitan areas. Apart from his wages his annual reward was either half a crown or a dozen at Christmas.

Ear basher: A pub bore.

Eat the horse, chase the rider: An expression shouted by a disappointed punter (a follower of racehorses) after his selection has *dipped out* or 'run out of the money'. He or she has 'done the rent' which will lead to an inevitable 'domestic' (punch up with one's spouse) later on in the day.

Face like a stopped clock: The person being referred to is either ugly, or stunned, or both.

Fair crack of the whip: Someone is not giving the utterer of the phrase a *fair go*, probably by drinking too fast or stealing the cocaine, thus the expression (uttered in outrage), '*Fair crack of the whip*, mate.'

Fair dinkum: The absolute truth as in, 'He's a *fair dinkum* bastard, *fair dinkum* he is, he's *fair dinkum*, my *bloody* oath.' As a general observation anyone who utters such a phrase can be regarded as, 'three sheets into the wind', 'pissed as a parrot' or, in plain English, drunk.

Fair go: Someone who is asking for a *fair crack of the whip*.

Fair suck of the sauce bottle: Another person who is not getting a *fair crack of the whip*.

Fart in a bottle: Someone is behaving like a... Farts are believed to behave somewhat oddly when contained in bottles.

Feather duster: A descriptive term normally confined to the future of politicians as in, 'This week he's top rooster but next week he'll be nothing but a *bloody feather duster*.' Although feather dusters have been made almost obsolete due to the invention of the vacuum cleaner the expression persists.

Feeding time at the zoo: Similar expression to 'shark feeding frenzy'. A scene of uncoordinated lunacy involving a large number of people. The behaviour of a group of Australians at a buffet table; bedlam and greed combined.

First cab off the rank: The person who is entitled to his or her reward because he or she is at the head of the queue. Sometimes this means that the person in question is the first to be sacked or shot. It has some similarity with the phrase, 'first up, best dressed'.

Floater: A meat pie which has been placed in a soup-plate full of mashed, dried, blue boiler peas and then topped with bottled tomato sauce. A favourite dish of people who live in the city of Adelaide, it has failed to rate a mention in *Larousse Gastronomique*.

Floating on ice: Drunk.

Form: In reference to racehorses if the four-footed idiot has 'good *form*' it may well win the race. If a human being is in 'good *form*' it means that he or she is witty and entertaining.

Fossick: To search for gold where others have failed to find it.

Four b' two: An unmetricated piece of timber which is widely used throughout the country to hammer sense into the skulls of dumb animals. Politicians are widely threatened with this treatment as in, 'You'd have to take an piece of *four b' two* to the bastard to make him see the sense of it.' An implement of discipline; a pick handle in the rough.

Fourpenny dark: Cheap red fortified wine, usually quite nasty.

Full as a: The start of many expressions; *'full as a* butcher's pup', *'full as a* goog' and *'full as a* state school' to name but three. All refer to the fact that the speaker is 'as pissed as a parrot'. Intoxicated.

Full bore: To go all out, to give one's best as in, 'He came at me *full bore* but I *stoushed* the *bastard* anyway.'

Furphy: An Australian-Irish expression meaning a lie as in, 'That's a *bloody furphy*, mate.' Singular only. No one in his or her right mind attempts to put over a bunch of furphies.

Galah: One of the more beautiful birds of Australia's dry areas with its rose-coloured breast, its impressive crests and its pink-grey wings. In flight a flock of galahs, although raucous, is sheer poetry. In human parlance, a *bloody* fool.

Get a bag: A cricketing term of abuse uttered by one sitting in the cheap seats. Means that the fielder to whom the abuse is directed has dropped an easy catch.

Get stuck into: A phrase meant to encourage one's mates to work hard, thus, 'If we *get stuck into* this lot right away we'll be down at the boozer in no time at all.'

Gibber: A stone or a small rock. Australia is famous in geological circles for its stoney or *gibber* deserts. European beaches are, to the astonishment of most Australians, mainly composed of *gibbers*.

Gin: A female Aborigine or lubra.

Ging: In the States of Western and South Australia a child's word for a shanghai which is called by its correct name by juveniles who dwell in the eastern part of the continent.

Give it a go: A term of encouragement sometimes translated as 'give it a

Get a bag:

burl'. Similar to *get stuck into* meaning once again that as soon as we all get together and get this job over and done with the quicker we can get to the boozer.

Give it a miss: Means that one is about to *dip out*, as in, 'Well I wouldn't mind going to the races with you but I'll cop it from the missus and so I think I'll *give it a miss* this time. But I'll catch up with you later.'

Go for the doctor: A racing term. If a horse has *gone for the doctor* it is about to win the race by a country mile.

Go under (someone's) neck: To take unfair advantage thus, 'I thought I had the job but the *bloody bastard went under me neck*.'

Goanna oil: A mythical oil made from the flesh of boiled down lizards who were doing no one any harm until the arrival of Europeans in the continent. It has the reputation of being able to eat its way through glass containers as well as being able to cure cancer. Entirely different from 'the good oil' which is a hot racing tip. Both oils are a load of rubbish.

God Botherer: A man of the cloth. A clergyman of the Christian persuasion.

Godzone: Short for Godzone Country; Australia.

Go for a burl: To take the family car out illegally for a high speed run involving the forces of law and order at some stage. After one has been for *a burl* one's father 'beats the shit' out of one.

Gone to the pack: Someone who has failed.

Good sort: A *grouse* looking *sheila*.

Got the game by the throat: In control of a given situation, as in, 'No worries, missus, the verandah'll be finished by tomorrow, we've *got the game by the throat.*'

Greenie: A rabid left-wing radical member of the alternative society who although violently opposed to the destruction of forests expects to get both his milk and his newspaper delivered daily.

Grouse: Good. One can have a '*grouse* feed' or a '*grouse* time'. A *sheila* can be *grouse* but a bloke never is.

Gurnsey: If one 'gets a *gurnsey*' or is given one, one is deemed to have succeeded in one's given task.

Had the claw: Something or someone is *buggered*. Normally used in reference to a piece of machinery which will no longer work as in, 'Sorry, mate, but your washing machine's *had the bloody claw.*' Pieces of machinery can also be deemed to have had the 'sword', 'Richard' or 'Dick'.

Happy as a bastard on father's day: Extremely unhappy.

Happy as Larry: Extremely happy, although God alone knows why the Larry's of this world should be in a continuous state of merriment.

Hard word: If one puts the *hard word* on a *sheila* one expects her to 'come across' — to have sexual intercourse. If one puts the *hard word* on one's mate one expects at least a tenner ($10).

Hatter: A solitary bushman, usually half mad. Although derived from the English phrase, 'as mad as a *hatter*' (because they were made mad by the use of mercury in the hat-making business), it has absolutely nothing to do with headgear.

Have a go: A sporting term meaning, 'Get stuck into it, you lazy bastard.'

Have a shot at: To attempt to take the piss out of someone else verbally as in, 'The bastard *had a shot at me* but I told him where he could get off. The bastard can go to buggery as far as I am concerned.'

Hawkesbury duck: An ear of maize or a corncob with the kernels intact. Road gang convicts used to steal these cobs from nearby farmers' fields when they thought they would not be detected. A derisory phrase meaning that one has very little to eat. Still used in the country to give vent to the feelings that one is hard up through no fault of one's own, thus if one is making one's dinner from *Hawkesbury duck* and 'underground mutton' there is 'sweet FA' in the house.

Hay, Hell and Booligal: The nasty end of the *Back of Beyond*. Nowhere, or the fag end of the universe, or as our great Aussie poet Banjo Paterson put it, 'the infernal regions of heat, dust and flies'. Normally uttered thus: 'I'm buggered if I know where he's gone, it's all *Hay, Hell and Booligal* here, mate.' In the literal sense the township of Hungerford on the New South Wales – Queensland border, being somewhat to the 'Back o' Bourke', is *Hay, Hell and Booligal* to a nicety.

Head on him like a robber's dog: Self-explanatory.

Hen's teeth: As scarce as. Even *Blind Freddy* knows that hens have no teeth.

Here's looking at you sideways: A verbal thank-you to a mate who has just shouted you to a schooner.

Hit the kapok: To state one's intention of going to bed to sleep. One can also state that one is going to 'Bungidoo', 'snatch a stretch of shut eye', 'somolosa' or express the intention of being about to be 'wrapped in the arms of Murphys'. For the sub-literate, Murphys is the Australianism of Morpheus.

Hit the nail on the head: To get to the nub of the matter.

Home and hosed: The racehorse or hayburner concerned has well and truly *gone for the doctor*. In political terms, 'The polls are closed and your loyal supporters are pissing it up in your opponent's office.' Someone has won something.

Hoon: A high-class dole bludger. An idiot.

Hoop: A jockey.

Hooroo: Literally goodbye, as in, 'Well *hooroo* then, I'll catch yer later.'

Hughie: God. Always used in, 'Send 'er down, *Hughie.*' Meaning, please God make it rain a lot. Why the Australian God should be called Hughie, rather than the Lord of Prophets or even Father Divine, has managed to exercise the minds of psychiatrists for some little time.

Humdinger: A 'little beauty'. Something very good or excellent, as in, 'You little *bloody humdinger* you, my oath.'

Hump the bluey: To carry the swag.

Humpy: A bark hut.

Hungry bastard: Someone who will stop at nothing to get an extra quid (dollar). Someone who would steal the stamp money from his blind mother. A shithead.

If it was raining palaces I'd get hit by the dunny door: One of a number of phrases meaning that one's never ever had a lucky streak or won a lottery.

Ikey Mo: A disparaging remark used to describe a member of the Jewish race. In its generality it means a moneylender.

Illywhacker: A smartarsed trickster.

If it was raining palaces I'd get hit by the dunny door:

In like Flynn: One is onto a sure thing. Refers to the now dead Hollywood-Australian film star Errol Flynn who, it was claimed, had his way with any woman of his choice. After his death a number of gutter journalists or Grubb Street hacks claimed that he was at least bi-, if not entirely homo-, sexual.

Jumbuck: A sheep. Normally used in reference to a ram.

Jump the rattler: To catch an illegal ride on a train, normally by hiding in an empty wheat car.

Kacky hander: One who writes and does everything else with his or her left hand. Otherwise an awkward bastard.

Kangaroos in the top paddock: One of many phrases indicating that someone is stark, raving mad. However, the person is a harmless madman. The person concerned can also be 'one sandwich off the full picnic'.

Kark: To '*chunder*', to have '*a technicolour yawn*', 'laugh at the ground' or '*shout for Ruth*'. But one can also *kark* which means to die. Therefore the person can be said to have *karked* it. Machinery, especially cars, can also *kark* it.

Kick on: To continue drinking after someone has 'found the necessary' or 'got the readies', meaning that one in the party has found enough money to buy the next round of drinks.

Kick the bucket: To die.

Kick the tin: To donate to a worthy cause especially to the widow of someone who has just *kicked the bucket*.

Killer: A bullock or sheep that has been reserved for eventual consumption on the homestead or station in the form of a *baked dinner*.

King hit: To knock someone down unfairly with a single blow, normally delivered without warning. If one has been *king hit* one has been knocked senseless. One can also be *kinged* which is the same thing.

Kiwi: A resident of New Zealand.

Knock back: To be rejected (normally by a woman) as in, 'I put the *hard word* on her but I got a *knock back*.'

Knocker: One who knocks. A critic as in, 'Every time I come up with a good idea the bastard *knocks* it.'

Knockers: The mammary glands of a human female. Tits.

Knuckle down: One who is prepared to *show willing*. If someone *knuckles down* to a job, he or she is deemed to be a good worker.

Knuckle sandwich: A 'bunch of fives' delivered in the direction of one's teeth. If one 'wears a *knuckle sandwich*', one is in a lot of trouble.

Lady's Waist:

Kybosh: If one 'puts the *kybosh*' on something, one is deemed to be a *knocker*. A bringer of bad luck.

Lady's Waist: This is the first and final entry in this dictionary of slang relating to beer measures. A Lady's Waist used to be either a 5- or 7-ounce measure of beer once served only in the parlour of a pub in New South Wales, but in Queensland was known as a glass because it was taken as a chaser to a glass or shot of neat rum. In New South Wales a schooner is somewhat short of a pint which is known as a pot in Victoria but in the aforementioned State a pint is a pint but never has been sold as such because there were no glasses to hold that measure. A pot used to be a 7-ounce in Western Australia where a schooner was 10 ounces, but in South Australia if you wanted a Coopers you had to ask for a bottle because only West End was sold in glasses or off the tap. In Tasmania a glass of Cascade is sold as a glass while in Queensland Fourex comes in stubbies or tinnies. Just ask for a beer.

Lair: A flash bastard who plays up like *billy-oh* and dresses up like a *pox doctor's clerk*. Normally anyone who is a *lair* is called a 'mug *lair*'. A show off. The Americanism is arsehole.

Larrikin: A poorly dressed mug *lair* who is prone to punch ups at the drop of a hat.

Leave you short: Invariably a question asked by a *cadger* or 'bot' who has just borrowed money. In a vague attempt to ease his conscience after he has grabbed the rent money he asks, 'Now are you sure that this won't *leave you short?*' It will.

Lick you to death: Derisory term for a watchdog that isn't. A failed blue heeler. The dog in question will.

Lie doggo: To keep one's head down while the shit is hitting the fan. To be extremely quiet.

Life wasn't meant to be easy: A phrase erroneously attributed to a right-wing prime minister of the 1970s, meaning that one was supposed to work for one's keep. It contradicted the universally held Marxist doctrine of the time that 'All men are born equal,' and concentrated on the end of the misquote, which goes, 'but everywhere they are in chains'. The prime minister in question wanted to make damn sure that the poor remained in chains. His ability as a statesman has been shown by the fact that despite the fact that his right-wing federal government has been overthrown, by one of (in theory) a leftist persuasion, the poor remain very firmly chained indeed and are likely to remain in this state for many years to come.

Like flies around a cow yard: An unpleasant phrase to describe Australian journalists clustering around a free drinks table.

Living daylights: If one has the *living daylights* scared out of one, one is very scared indeed.

Long streak of cocky's shit: A reference to someone who is both very tall and very arrogant. The phrase, 'long streak of pelican's shit' means the same thing. Normally uttered by short people who feel inferior.

Lord Muck: An expression of abuse as in '*bloody Lord Muck* of Shit Hall'. The person uttering the phrase is in effect stating that someone has risen above his or her station in life and has adopted the affectations of the English nobility. But he or she has buggered it up and cannot understand the use of snail tongs let alone the *doover* for asparagus. A mug *lair* in fancy dress and language.

Lousy: One is 'crook in the guts' or otherwise off-colour.

Lower than a snake's belly: The person is. A dead-set bastard.

Lubra: A female Aborigine.

Lunatic soup: Alcohol in any form. Normally uttered by a police spokesman as in, 'Well, we could contain them until the bastards really got stuck into the *lunatic soup*.'

Mad as a cut snake: Both crazy and angry. Any Australian snake which has been cut in half doesn't take kindly to its aggressor.

Madwoman's breakfast/knitting/lunch: In a dreadful mess. Mad women are deemed to be somewhat sloppy by the general populace.

Mag: To talk to another, as in, 'We had a good *mag*.'

Makings: If one asks for the *makings* one expects to receive in return a packet of fine-cut tobacco, cigarette papers and a box of matches, hence the query, 'You wouldn't have the *makings* about you, mate, would you?'

Man with the Minties: A tipster or a sleevetugger who tips you a horse which promptly loses, thus, 'I was going to back Phar Lap but I met the *Man with the Minties*.'

Marvel: As in the statement, 'You're a *bloody marvel*; I hope they can breed off you.' A sarcastic remark directed at someone who has buggered things up.

Matilda: An assortment of one's personal possesssions rolled up in a blanket. If one goes 'Waltzing *Matilda*', in the words of the national song, one is deemed to be 'humping the bluey on the *Wallaby*'.

Met fairy: A meteorologist, because, 'they're always playing with balloons'.

Metho: A drinker of methylated spirits. A derelict.

Moggy: A cat.

Motza: If one scores a *motza* one has won a packet. To win the lottery or otherwise be in luck.

Mozzy: The plural of the word is *mozzies*. Mosquitoes which are as big as pigs and have tusks as well.

Muddie: Short for Queensland mud crab. The best eating crab along Australia's shores. Anything of the crustacean variety that is not a *muddie* is regarded as being 'good only for shark bait'.

Mulga: If one is 'in the *mulga*' one is in a particularly obnoxious part of the Australian outback where the beer is warm. The scrub.

Mullock: To 'poke *mullock*' means to 'poke borak'. To insult. One can also be 'in the *mullock*' which is the same as being in the shit.

Mullygrubber: A low and unfair ball bowled underarm in cricket.

My oath: A reply to almost anything as in: 'It's a hot day.' '*My oath*.' 'It's a cold day.' '*My oath*.' 'Would you like a drink?' '*My oath*.' 'How's about going up the Cross and getting on the piss and picking up a coupla *sheilas?*' '*My bloody oath*.' The phrase used to be known as 'my colonial oath' but since Federation the word 'colonial' has been dropped.

Nark: A wet blanket. Someone who *knocks* or criticises as in, 'He's nothing but a *bloody nark*.' In a secondary sense it also means one who constantly criticises but is not prepared to lend a hand to put things to rights.

Nasho: One who in past years was forced to serve his country for his country's good. Short for National Serviceman.

Ned Kelly: A misguided socialist of vague Irish descent who was stupid enough (thanks to his Irish ancestry) to make a mere half suit of armour, thus allowing the forces of law and order to shoot and capture him. He was then hanged for his stupidity. Before dying he did *not* utter the words, 'Such, such is life'; a reporter from the Melbourne *Age* newspaper did. Because of this misguided dottiness Ned Kelly has become Australia's folk hero giving rise to the phrase, 'as game as *Ned Kelly*'. The variant of the phrase is 'as game as Phar Lap'. Phar Lap was a horse.

Never Never: Home of the outback Aborigines, meaning the desert regions of Australia. A somewhat affectionate term for the country that is deemed to be 'beyond the *Black Stump*'.

Nipper: Either a small freshwater crustacean or a child above the *rug rat* stage. Never used in the female sense. A small boy who *shows willing* or is said to be useful is held to be, 'a handy little *nipper*'.

No bloody picnic: One has emerged from a situation of almost total disaster but one is not about to admit it. Thus in reply to the question, 'Well, how'd it go then?', the correct Australian male answer is, 'Well, it was *no bloody picnic.*'

No hoper: A fool.

No worries: A terrifying phrase meaning usually that the house is going to fall down, as in *'No worries,* missus, she'll be sweet.' Having said this the builder departs and the house does indeed fall down.

Norks: A woman's breasts. The origin is uncertain; possibly from the Norco butter wrappings which show a cow's udder.

Not half bad: Extra *grouse.* Thus the correct reply to the question as to whether one likes the vintage champagne, is, 'Well, it's *not half bad.'* This means that the product in question is excellent.

Not the full bottle: Means that someone is 'not the full quid' (archaic) or has *kangaroos in his or her top paddock.* One of a number of phrases meaning that the person in question is 'two bricks short of a load' or that 'You can knock but no one answers.'

Not worth a bumper/not worth a crumpet: Worthless. Bumpers being fag ends are indeed worthless, but crumpets being a form of griddle cake with holes are quite tasty. This therefore is a silly and meaningless expression.

Ocker: The average Australian male usually called Norm, Alf or Bruce. His going-out rig consists of a T-shirt, shorts, thongs and an Esky full of tinnies.

Off his (or her) face: Mad.

Off like a bride's nightie: To depart quickly.

Off the hook: Safe. If one has managed to get one's self *off the hook* one has managed to avoid a difficult situation which means that usually one has told a barefaced lie.

Oldie: A word used by one under the age of 17 for anyone over the age of 20.

On the nose: Off; literally bad smelling. Usually used in reference to a shady deal which is held to be *on the nose*.

On the outer: If one is *on the outer* one is normally forced to *drink with the flies*. A position of being a temporary outcast.

Over the odds: A 'bit rough'. Normally said of one who is deemed to be 'coming on a bit strong'. A statement that is a palpable lie.

Paddington Leftie: An upwardly and greedily mobile 'parlour' socialite. Somewhat the same as a *basketweaver from Balmain* but richer. The Americanisms are WASP and Yuppie.

Pantywaist: A male who is not necessarily homosexual but someone who nevertheless is regarded as a sissy in the old-fashioned sense.

Pass muster: To be acceptable. Anyone who *passes muster* can from that time on be regarded as a good bloke. One who accepts responsibilities.

Petrolhead:

Pearler: You little beauty. Very good.

Perve: In its most general sense the male habit of eyeing up a woman. However, a *perve* or someone thus named is a child molester.

Petrolhead: One who is obsessed by his or her car far and beyond the medallion of the Blessed Virgin and the pyjama puppy in the back seat behind the venetian blinds. One who decorates his or her car in the taste of idiocy.

Phoney: Normally used in the somewhat archaic phrase '*phoney* as a two bob watch', meaning that the person being referred to is a trickster or otherwise dud. Always used in reference to bipeds and never when talking about inanimate objects.

Piccaninny: An Aboriginal child.

Piccaninny daylight: Shepherd's or false dawn.

Pie eater: A person of no consequence. A dickhead.

Piece: Of Western and Southern Australian origin now found only in the realms of literature by those authors who are attempting to be stylishly nationalistic. The literal translation is 'a piece of bread, jam and butter'. A young child was normally given a *piece* when he or she came home from school. Nowdays they are either given a Fanta and a bickie or they go out and buy themselves a snort of coke with Mum's sherry money.

Pig Iron Bob: An obscure and more than somewhat fat leader of the Australian Federation in the 1950s and 1960s who fancied himself in double-breasted suits. His phrase-making fame came from the fact that he sold a lot of scrap iron to the Japanese empire shortly before the start of a minor matter known as World War II. The Japanese empire returned this favour in the form of shells, hence the phrase *Pig Iron Bob*. His full name was Robert Gordon Menzies.

Piss in the same pot: The same as 'pee in the same pot' which is very nearly the same as the Americanism to whit, 'to piss in someone's pocket', or, to use another Americanism, in a slightly different sense, 'to have his pecker in my pocket' (Lyndon Baines Johnson, circa 1978). In general terms to be a crawler or to suck up to someone.

Piss poor: A poor show. The horse performed badly.

Pitt Street Farmer: A Sydney expression which had some original sense when all the banks were in Pitt Street of that city. Means that someone is using country property losses for city advantages. The Melbourne expression is Collins Street Farmer.

Plonk: Cheap wine. One who is a *plonko* gets drunk on the stuff.

Poddy-dodger: A cattle stealer who specialises in calves. A cattle duffer who confines his activities to immature beasts.

Pointing Percy at the porcelain: To take a leak, have a piss. To urinate.

Polly: A parrot or a politician. The definitions are similar.

Possum: An Australian term of endearment, as in 'You litle *possum*, you.' Something soft and cuddly. Unfortunately Australian possums are anything but cuddly, having razor sharp claws.

Poultice: If one 'puts a *poultice*' on something one has invested a serious amount of money (usually on a horse).

Pox doctor's clerk: If one is dressed up in the fashion of a *pox doctor's clerk* one is deemed to be overdressed, out of character or *lairy*. One is also probably in actual fact a 'mug *lair*.' 'Arse about sideways' in other words.

Pub: An hotel.

Puftaloon: A fried version of damper served with *Cocky's Joy*. Puftaloons were often fried in deep mutton fat. This combination at times caused death. Amazingly enough, in past years many bushmen regarded puftaloons as excellent puddin'.

Pull your head in: Shut up.

Punch the bundy: Literally to arrive at work on time and check in at one's appointed hour. However, in popular parlance *punching the bundy* meant that one was unwillingly doing a lot of 'hard *graft*' in an effort to 'make a *quid*'.

Push: Member of a sect. Now somewhat archaic except in the sense of 'a member of the literary *push*'. Members of a *push* were once regarded as larrikins or 'street stoushers'. The Australian word for a street gang.

Put the bite on: To ask for a loan of money.

Put the mockers on: To wish or cause bad luck. Anyone who *puts the mockers* on something is a dead-set *bastard*.

Quid: Formerly a one pound note, still occasionally heard in the phrase 'not worth a bloody *quid*' (worthless), or 'not the full *quid*' (insane).

Rabbit: Used by either male or female about another male who is held to be weak, normally in the phrase, he's a 'bit of a *rabbit*'. Rabbits also have the distressing tendency to *rabbit on*; to talk about nothing at all over an interminable period of time whereupon they are told to 'stop rabbiting'. On the other hand a 'rabbitoh' (now archaic) was one who sold rabbits for a living from door to door. He was normally accompanied by a mate who sold clothes props which were not used to prop up clothes, but rather the line that held the said garments on washing day.

Rage: A sort of late-night perambulating party involving anyone from the sub-teen acne set through punks and dole-bludging hippies to Yuppies. Normally involves grog, the acceptable social drugs of the day and a little statutory fornication. Not half as much fun as the old-fashioned *rort* or *shivoo* which not only involved all of the above but serious fist fights as well.

Rapt: If one is *rapt* in something it is really good.

Rat up a rope: If one does something like a *rat up a rope* one has moved exceedingly quickly.

Ratbag: The bush version of a *dickhead*.

Rattler: A train. If one 'jumps the *rattler*' one hides in a cattle truck to avoid paying one's fare.

Raw Prawn: If someone 'comes the *raw prawn*', one has behaved in an extremely offensive fashion, hence, 'Don't come the *bloody raw prawn* with me, mate.'

Real drop kick: Someone who is a real *droob* or nerd (American: wimp), with the added disadvantage that he or she is probably on hard drugs.

Real Yarra: Slightly older version of the above phrase meaning that the person is boring and muddy or unclear, in reference to the River Yarra which runs through the city of Melbourne.

Reds under the bed: All right-thinking middle class Australians are terrified of finding reds (or communists) either under the bed or dominating the unions and running the country. The fear actually has nothing to do with the rise of the Soviet Communist Party. Australians have constantly feared invasion by the Soviet Union since the days of the Tsar. The country's coastline is littered with useless nineteenth-century forts that were built to thwart this. This is despite the fact that the northern and frozen nation has shown no interest whatsoever in claiming Ayers Rock as its own. The phrase *reds under the bed* is now used as a term of derision by members of the Labor Party's left wing when their political opponents are kicking up a stink about something or other.

Ridgie didge: On the level; the good oil. The truth.

Ringer: The fastest shearer in the shed. Also known as the gun or gun shearer.

Ripper: An expression of joy. If someone shouts, 'You little *ripper*', it means that his horse has won the race.

Room in a railway station: An unusual but not archaic phrase meaning that someone is down on his or her luck. The only place to sleep is the waiting room of a railway station.

Rort: An enjoyable party with dancing and violence (and of course grog).

Rough as guts: A bad turn, a piece of bad sportsmanship or a deliberately nasty act, as in 'Did you see what the *bastard* did? That was as *rough as guts.*'

Rough end of the stick: Someone has had the dirty done on him or her and is thus left holding the *rough end of the stick*.

Rouseabout: A general hand in a shearing shed.

Rubbity: Short for *rubbity dub* — a pub or an hotel.

Rug rat: A small and obnoxious child under two years of age.

Saltbush: Marginal and virtually useless sheep-grazing country invariably settled by battlers, such as the cartoon character Saltbush Bill. Anyone in the bush who is known locally as Saltbush Bill is regarded as a failure.

Salvo: A member of the Salvation Army of either sex. A female Salvationist is sometimes called a Sally Anne.

Sandy Blight: An eye infection suffered by someone living in the interior of Australia. The eye disease, trachoma.

Sanger: A sandwich.

Sarky: Bad tempered, as in, 'Don't get *sarky* with me you *bastard*.'

Sav: Short for a largish dyed sausage known as a saveloy, which is a sort of inflated frankfurter or hot dog. A battered sav on a stick (for the uninitiated: a saveloy covered in a flour and water paste, impaled on a popsicle bat and then deep fried) is still an esteemed Australian fair ground snack. This culinary horror is invariably dipped in tomato sauce before being thrust into the fingers of the unwary.

Scorcher: A bloody hot day. A 'real' *scorcher* is a *bastard*.

Scrub round it: To avoid or disregard a problem, thus, this exchange:
'Hey Mate! the roof's about to fall in.'
'Don't worry mate, we'll just *scrub round it* and *she'll be Jake* in no time at all.'

Scrub up well: If one *scrubs up well* one is deemed by one's peers to have managed to get dressed quite decently and look *not half bad* after an appalling night on the *turps*. Also some women are said by males to *scrub up well* which simply means that they have dress sense. This is merely thought and not uttered.

Scrubber: A cow or steer that has gone wild in the scrub. An ugly woman.

See yer later: A typical Australianism which does not mean that the one who utters the phrase has any intention whatsoever of meeting the person in question at a future date. It simply means goodbye. Confusing to foreigners.

Selection: A land grant. Now found only in nationalistic literature and starting with the words, 'Things were crook on our selection...' The worst selection in Australia was farmed by the literary figures of Dad and Dave who were the heroic battlers of Steele Rudd's *On Our Selection* and *On Our New Selection*.

Shagged: Exhausted from hard work.

Shake hands with the wife's best friend: A lengthy male euphemism for the act of urination, normally prefaced by, 'Hang on a minute, I'm just going to...'

Sharkbait: A stupid swimmer who body surfs or swims in dangerous areas encouraging attacks by sharks.

Sheila: A member of the female sex. In these days of chairpersons there is no modern equivalent.

She's Jake: An expression meaning that things are all right, which they are not.

Shicker: If one gets 'on the *shicker*' one intends to get drunk, hence *shickered*.

Shirt tearing: A form of male pub fighting in which no one is intended to get hurt and no one does. In retrospect normally spoken of with disgust. 'It was nothing but a bunch of *shirt tearing*.'

Shivoo: A party similar to a *rort* except that in the first instance dancing takes precedence over fighting.

Shonky: Goods of poor quality or a job that has been badly done.

Shoosh: A demand for an audience to shut up, as in , 'Let's have a bit of *shoosh*, ladies and gents.'

Shot through like a Bondi tram: Somewhat archaic although still in use by those who remember the days of Sydney trams with affection. The Bondi tram was notoriously the most dangerous and fastest. It means therefore that the person in question has 'pissed off at the high port' or fled very quickly indeed.

Shouse: Something not very nice. Short for shithouse.

Shout: To stand a round in a school of drinkers in a pub, hence, 'It's my *shout*.' One whose turn it is to *shout* is said to be 'in the chair'.

Shout for Ruth: To go for the 'big spit'. To vomit.

Show willing: To indicate that one is prepared to either work hard or fend for one's self as best one can. One *shows willing* if one is going to *crack hardy*.

Sickie: If one 'takes a *sickie*' one pretends one is ill while actually attending the races. To sadly misplace the trust and generosity of one's employer.

Shout for Ruth:

Silvertail: A member of the upper classes or anyone who is richer than the person making the accusation. The adjective *bloody* normally precedes the use of the word.

Sin Bin: A place where a sportsman is sent after being ordered off the field for appalling behaviour.

Sit up like Jacky: To brightly and conspicuously pay attention to what one is being told. In the main, dogs and children *sit up like Jacky*. Adults seldom do.

Skerrick: If there is 'not a *skerrick* left' there is nothing. Normally spoken by people who arrive late for a beer and prawn night after everyone else has had a good time.

Skite: To boast.

Sleepout: A half-enclosed verandah where male guests and dogs can doss down for the night. The forerunner of the granny flat.

Smell of an oil rag: An expression applied to any newcomer to Australia if she or he works hard and does well. People who are said to be able to 'live off the *smell of an oil rag*' are those who, in other words, sacrifice present comfort to future prosperity.

Smoko: The manual worker's morning or afternoon tea break. Rigidly enforced by the unions it is much frowned upon by captains of industry.

Smoodge: An attempt to ingratiate one's self. Used mainly to animals as in 'Don't come *smoodging* round here, you'll get nothing to eat from me.'

Snaffle: To pinch or thieve but in a minor and harmless fashion. One might *snaffle a sanger* from a buffet table, but one definitely steals a full bottle of Scotch.

Snags: Snorkers or sausages. Rarely if ever used in the singular form.

Snake's piss: Bad alcohol.

Snaky: Irritable.

Sool: To encourage one dog to attack either another dog, animal or person as in, 'Go on then, get into 'im, *sool* the *bastard*.' The dog in question is encouraged to do serious injury, if not cause actual death.

Spinner: The person tossing the coins in a game of two up, an Australian gambling game once played with two imperial copper pennies.

Spit chips: To be so annoyed that one is capable of chewing up logs of wood and *spitting chips*.

Squattocracy: A member of the colonial landholding aristocracy. A rich land owner. Derisive term.

Starve the lizards: An expression of amazement or incredulity. A downmarket version of the English expression, By Jove!

Sticks out like dog's balls: It does.

Stipe: A stipendary steward at a horseracing meeting, who, sitting in judgment with his peers, has the ability to disqualify a jockey or warn a gambler off the course for life.

Stir the possum: To creat uproar. Native possums when sleeping in a hollow log react violently when poked with a stick — hence the phrase.

Stirrer: One who sets out to deliberately cause trouble and discontent. Shop floor stewards and members of the left-wing faction of the Australian Labor Party are normally branded as stirrers even if they are attempting to be quite agreeable at the time.

Stone the crows: Used in conjunction with *starve the lizards* or by itself as an expression of amazement about either good or bad events. In actuality both expressions have no meaning whatsoever.

Stoush: A punch up or a fight.

Strewth!: A short and supposedly decent form of the old English phrases, God's Teeth! and God's Truth! It gave the utterer the right to blaspheme without actually appearing to do so.

Strides: Trousers, as in the phrase, 'Be right with you as soon as I get me *strides* on.'

Strike a light: An expression of very little meaning usually inserted at the beginning of a sentence simply to give the speaker time to collect his thoughts as in, '*Strike a light*, but she's a bloody beaut day.'

Strike me pink: The Australian version of the English, 'fancy that'. Something unusual has happened, usually pleasant.

Strong: As in, 'What's the *strong* of this?', meaning, 'What in the name of hell is going on?' If used in the personal sense it is normally expressed as, 'What's the *strength* of that bastard?', meaning, 'What is the swine up to?'

Stroppy: Someone who is *stroppy* is in a bad temper.

Stubby: A small Australian beer bottle. Never used in reference to imported beers even if they do come in stubbies.

Stunned mullet: If someone has an expresssion like a *stunned mullet* that person is deemed to be both ugly and stupid. However, the Antipodean mullet is an excellent, if somewhat oily, eating fish.

Sundowner: A scruffier version of the normal swagman, inasmuch as although the normal swagman would arrive in time to split a load of wood in order to get his tucker ration, the sundowner deliberately arrived at a station or homestead at dusk so that any thought of work was impossible.

Suss: To search out, thus to '*suss* out'.

Susso: The pre-World War II version of the dole. 'On the *susso*' was an expression of derision used by *silvertails*, and one of defiance by those on it. Technically one who is receiving a government handout.

Swag: A bedroll containing one's personal possessions and carried by the means of two straps. Balanced on one shoulder only, with a flour sack, termed a tucker bag, used as a counter-balance in front. One of the easiest packs to carry for long distances.

Swagman, swaggie: One who carries a swag. A wanderer. Not much seen walking these days as most swaggies have the brains to hitch rides on 'big rigs'.

Swan: One can either be 'on a *swan*' or '*swanning around*'. Swanning is loafing, although if one is swanning around one is a travelling loafer or *swaggie*. To confuse the issue if one '*swans* around all day' it usually means one has had an agreeable time at several different boozers. Swanning around at work means hiding in the bog.

Talk under wet cement with a mouthful of marbles:

Tailormade: A packet or manufactured cigarette which is purchased in its pristine entirety as distinct from a 'rollie' which is a roll-your-own cigarette put together from the *makings*.

Take a powder: To piss off, shoot through, disappear in a hurry. Normally one *takes a powder* when the 'wallopers' are after one.

Take a shine to: To take a liking to someone.

Talk under wet cement with a mouthful of marbles: A pub bore whom no one can shut up.

Talk you blind: The same pub bore who does. An ear basher.

Tall poppy: Any Australian who reads more than the sporting results and knows how to use snail tongs. Someone who aspires to intellectual excellence and cannot tell the difference between one make of car and another. The species is much hated in Australia and is always being cut down to size.

This last act is the main reason why the country always will suffer from intellectual cretinism.

Tank: The word used west of the Darling River in New South Wales, and in the dead heart, for a dam.

Technicolour yawn: To vomit.

The middle of the bloody day and not a bone in the truck: Nothing has been achieved despite a fair amount of striving.

Things are crook in Tallarook: Matters are not reaching any satisfactory conclusion, the times are bad and everything is up shit creek. Apart from that the phrase has no meaning whatsoever; it is just something to say during a lull in the conversation.

Thirty-seven degrees in the water bag: A hot day. One of the few succesful translations from the imperial to the metric measurement of temperature, indicating that the liquid in the canvas water bag is at blood heat.

Tick: If one gets something on *tick* one is getting one's beer on the slate or on credit.

Tickets on himself: If a male has *tickets on himself* he is regarded as a lairy stuck-up *bastard*. Someone who believes himself to be smarter than he actually is.

Tickle the Peter; Someone who *tickles the Peter* is a minor thief. The English equivalent is a 'poor box John'.

Tiger country: Rough scrub with strong reference to the south west of Tasmania, the last known area in Australia where the Tasmanian tiger or thylacine was sighted.

Tight as a fish's arse: A mean bastard who won't lend you a *quid*.

Timid fish: Someone who does not like hard work.

Tin arsed: Lucky, although why one who is so smiled upon by Dame Fortune should have a bottom made of tin is beyond human understanding.

Tinned dog: Corned beef or mutton. Derisive.

Tinny: A can of beer, sometimes known as a tube.

Tired and emotional: Blind drunk. A euphemism once much used in the public prints for politicians who were 'three sheets in the wind' or otherwise 'pissed as parrots', to avoid the laws of libel.

Tissue: A Tasmanian term for a cigarette paper.

Toecutter: A standover man who literally chops people's feet off to indicate, in a jovial fashion, that they have rather stepped out of line. In the political terminology one who is extremely ruthless.

Top night: One has been blind drunk. One generally has a *top night* in the company of friends whereas one can get *shickered* by one's self.

Trimmer: If someone is said to be 'a little *trimmer*' he, she or it has done well. Normally used in reference to a horse or a dog that has won a race, but an inanimate object such as a lottery win can be held to be a little *trimmer* as well.

Troppo: Round the twist. Usually used of people who have gone insane in a tropical or sub-tropical environment.

Tuckerbox: Something that some damn fool of a dog sat on once near the New South Wales town of Gundagai. He was guarding this box of food for the return of his master. As his master was dead, the dog starved to death itself and the food in the box went bad. This tale of needless and stupid self-sacrifice by a brainless animal is very close to the Australian psyche, about as close in fact, as the charge of the Light Brigade is to the British. Dog, tuckerbox and the town of Gundagai have been enshrined in a bush ballad for many years. In short, a lunch pail.

Turps: If one is on the *turps* one is in the process of getting drunk.

Two pot screamer: A cheap drunk; someone who can get sloshed on two glasses of beer.

Two up: Once the national game played with a pair of pennies thrown into the air by a spinner. Now, thanks to the introduction of legalised casinos, the game is now on the wane and the State rather than the individual benefits.

Tyke: A derogatory term for a Catholic; the opposite end of the religious spectrum to the 'Proddy dog'.

Under the weather: Crook in the guts. Ill.

Underground chicken: Rabbit. In recent years this phrase has been mistranslated as 'underground mutton'. In poor families rabbit was often substituted for chicken in pies and other dishes because of the similarity of taste. Nothing can be substituted for the taste of Australian mutton. It is unique.

Up a gumtree: On the wrong track. To follow the wrong lead and therefore finish *up a gumtree*.

Up the duff: In a female sense, to be 'in the club'. Pregnant.

Up there, Cazaly: Triumphant term used by barrackers or supporters in the game of Australian Rules. Now more or less replaced by the boring phrase, 'go for it'. An encouragement for someone on the field to actually catch the ball.

Up who: Short form of 'who's *up who* and who's paying the rent?' An expression of general bewilderment in a bewildering situation; one where no one is in control and matters are entirely out of hand.

Up you for the rent: Abusive term meaning go and get stuffed thus, 'and when he put the hard word on me for a loan I told him, *up you for the rent, mate.*'

Urger: Racecourse tout or tipster. A term, generally of insult, as in, 'That bastard, he's nothing but a *bloody urger.*'

Ute: Short form of utility. Before the invention of the highly expensive four-wheel-drive vehicle with computer radar the most useful vehicle in the bush. By law all utes must contain at least one slavering blue heeler.

Vag: A vagrant; someone who is down on his luck. If one is *vagged* it means that one has been arrested by the 'wallopers' for having no visible means of support, or merely because they feel you are a stroppy *bastard*.

Virgin's ruin: Although in international parlance this is held to be gin, in Australia, Bundaberg rum, generally known as 'a bundi', is said to do the trick.

Wallaby Track: A path to the interior of the continent taken by failures. Successful people do not walk the *Wallaby Track*, they fly over it. If someone is said to be, 'off on the *Wallaby*' it is assumed that he is roaming the countryside looking for work.

Waltzing Matilda: Literally to carry one's swag along the *Wallaby Track*. The title of a rather odd jingle that almost everyone else in the civilised world fervently believes is the Australian national anthem. Quite a number of Australians think so as well.

Wanker: The literal translation is mental masturbator. Someone who is having himself on, thinks he's pretty good, and doesn't really know what he is talking about.

Warby: Used only in Western and South Australia for a *dero* or derelict with the added inference that the person is male, an alcoholic and one who picks up young Aboriginal girls.

Water burner: A bush or shearer's cook.

Watering hole: One's favourite pub.

Wax: A word used by juveniles meaning to share.

Weak: Short for 'piss *weak*' or '*weak* as cold piss on a plate'. The person being referred to is a doddering idiot.

Weekend warrior: A member of the Australian Army's Reservist units. The term is intended to be derogatory and is a variant on 'cut lunch commando'. Most Australian males prefer to defend their country at weekends from the redoubts of the nearest public bar.

Well heeled: A 'flash *bastard*' who's got more money than sense. However, he might be good for a 'bite' (loan).

Wet blanket: A killjoy.

Whack up: To share out. One *whacks up* the proceeds of a betting syndicate that has just won on the races.

Whacker: A person of no consequence; a fool.

Whacko: An expression of joy as in, '*Whacko*, we've just won the dozen of beer in the pub raffle.' Anything more *whacko* than *whacko* is '*whacko* the diddle-o' or '*whacko* the chook'.

Wharfie: Short for waterside worker. In international terms a stevedore.

What's the strength: Roughly, what in the name of hell is happening? But it can also be a query about a person's character, as in, *'What's the strength of that bastard* over there? Is he on the level or is he just putting us on?'

Where the crows fly backwards: The *Back of Beyond* or *Woop Woop*. In areas such as these the crows are forced to fly backwards to keep the dust out of their eyes.

White ant: To destroy another's character by slanderous and probably truthful gossip normally expressed thus, 'I was doing all right with the *sheila* until the bastard *white anted* me.'

White leghorn: A female lawn bowler. The standard dress for a woman who is a member of a lawn bowl team is white hat, white blouse, white skirt, white stockings and white shoes. Hence they are named after the well-known chook.

Who's robbing this coach?: A warning to someone to mind their own business which comes from the rather tired pub joke which goes:
Ned Kelly held up the mail coach, ordered all the passengers to get down into the road and then stated, 'I'm going to rob all the men and rape all the women.'
One gentleman intervened and said he would be damned if the blackguard would be allowed to carry out his intentions in regard to the ladies of the company. At that point one female piped up, *'Who's robbing this coach,* you or Mr Kelly?'

Wood duck: Technically the Australian *wood duck* is classified as a maned goose. Thus anyone who is called a *wood duck* is a goose. An idiot.

Woop Woop: Where the crows fly backwards or 'the arse end of nowhere'.

Wouldn't know: The start of a number of expresssions all of which mean stupidity. Thus, *'wouldn't know* it from a bull's foot', *'wouldn't know* if his arse was on fire', *'wouldn't know* if a band were up him until he got the drum'.

Wouldn't read about it: Something both unusual and unfortunate has just taken place as in, 'I thought we were home and hosed, but you *wouldn't* *read about it* the boss came round the corner of the shed and caught us with the lot. Unreal, it was.'

Wouldn't shout if a shark bit him: The person referred to shows a marked reluctance to stand his 'round' in the public bar 'school' and is seldom, if ever, in the 'chair'. An SOB who won't buy you a drink.

Wouldn't work in an iron lung: The person in question would indeed not. Exceedingly lazy.

Wowser: A non-drinking Christian who also attempts to get pornographic movies banned and regards the works of Shakespeare as suspect due to certain erotic passages.

Xenophobe: A standard male Anglo-Saxon Australian who is probably on the dole.

Yabbie: A freshwater crayfish despised by Australians and esteemed by dirty foreigners.

Yacker: Work. Most work is 'hard *yacker*'.

Yarn: If one 'has a *yarn*', one engages in conversation with another. But one can also tell or 'spin a *yarn*' which means that one is a teller of tales or stories. Most yarn spinners are bloody great liars.

Yellow Peril: An all embracing term that once covered the hordes of Asians that were poised to take over the country from the rightful grasp of the European Protestant invaders of the late eighteenth century. Almost as feared as the Red Menace.

You can't walk on one leg: The person who has just uttered the phrase has, after having consumed one drink, accepted the offer of a second, offered to him by his kind companion. A roundabout and needlessly complicated way of saying, 'Yes, thanks'.

You don't have to be dead to be stiff: Meaning that one can have a run of bad luck under almost any circumstances and for no good reason, the word *stiff* equals bad luck. '*Stiff* cheddar' is an Australianism for the English phrase, 'Hard cheese, old chap.' In coarser and more unfeeling circles it is sometimes translated as '*Stiff* shit, mate.'

You tell him, I stutter: This translates as, 'I am sick and tired of attempting to explain the facts of life to this fool here, so you have a go at it because I can be no longer bothered.' The person who has just abandoned explaining does not stutter and has never been known to; the *I stutter* being included to show total contempt.

You wouldn't be dead for quids: Something amazing and amusing (normally involving another's misfortune) has just occurred thus making thoughts of suicide, for the time being at least, unnecessary.

You're not wrong: The Australian way of saying, 'You are right.'

You're right: The Australian version of the Americanism, 'You're welcome.' Sometimes rendered as either, 'she's sweet' or '*no worries*'.

You've got to be in it to win it: If one doesn't buy a ticket in the lottery one doesn't 'stand a show' of collecting first prize. Self-explanatory.

Youze: The plural version of the singular you, as in 'see *youze*', which in itself means goodbye. *Youze* can be one person or many.

Zambuck: A voluntary or paid first aid or ambulance officer of either sex present at a sporting event. The name comes from a now long-forgotten healing cream that was once applied to wounds.